Make Someone Smile

30 Ways To Make A Person's Day Better

DR. VICKI ELLIS HARGROVE

STRATTON PRESS
Publishing Life

MAKE SOMEONE SMILE
Copyright © 2019 **Dr. Vicki Ellis Hargrove**

All rights reserved. No part of this book may be used or reproduced by any means, graphic, electronic, or mechanical, including photocopying, recording, taping or by information storage and retrieval system without the written permission of the author except in the case of brief quotations embodied in critical articles and reviews.

Stratton Press Publishing,
831 N Tatnall Street Suite M
#188, Wilmington, DE 19801
www.stratton-press.com
1-888-323-7009

Because of the dynamic nature of the Internet, any web addresses or links contained in this book may have changed since publication and may no longer be valid. The views expressed in the work are solely those of the author and do not necessarily reflect the views of the publisher, and the publisher hereby disclaims any responsibility for them.

ISBN (Paperback): 978-1-64345-322-4
ISBN (Ebook): 978-1-64345-417-7

Printed in the United States of America

To my grandchildren
and everyone who can make
someone else's day better

What did you do to make someone smile today?

1. Did you say "Good morning" to your…

Teacher   **Boss**

Co-Workers

Friends

Family

Bonjour
Guten Morgen
Buongiorno
Bom día
Günaydin
Buenos días

Aloha Kakahiaka
Goedemorgen
Sabah alkhyr
Selamat pagi
Dobroye utro

It is amazing how such a small statement can make someone's day.

2. Did you say "Thank you" to the person helping you?

Spasiba	Obrigado
Shukraan Jazilaan	Gracias
Dank U	Khop Khun Kha(p)
Merci	Arigatō
Danke	Takk
Mahalo	Kamsa hamnida
Toda	Salamat
Grazie	Cheers
Xièxiè	

They like to hear you noticed
what they did for you.

3. What did you do for the person having a bad day?

Did you show you cared?
Did you ask about his or her day?
Did you give him or her a hug?

4. How did you make the lonely person become part of your day?

Did you invite him or her to sit with you?
Did you ask about his or her day?
Did you introduce him or
her to your friends?
Did you eat lunch with him or her?
Did you sit down beside
him or her and talk?

5. Did you say "Hello" to the person on the street?

Bonjour   Ni Hau   Hola   Ciao
Guten Tag   Ola   Salaam
Ohayo   Marhaba

Everyone likes to be acknowledged.

6. Did you use the person's name?

Phyllis Ryan Hope Janice Ambur Bob Grayson Macey Mick Charlene Taylor Eliza Molly Ian Roshella Ellie Lila Puchi Griffin Ethan Betty Conner Brinn Stefanie TC Payne Kate Monolo Hayden Eloise Ann Greta Boyd Bennett RODNEY Jamey Karen Parker Connie Rae Nannette Greta Carl Shelley Vicki Katie Catherine Maria Mutsumi Zamyiah Rosa Nico Lorena Patricia Anselmo Ronnie Greg Stephen Colin Dianne Eddy Tonda Aspen Tina Gwynn Karin Marlene Ella Amy Fred Lauren Peter Mandee Theresa Von Denise Piper Dixie Warren Kevin Nancy Barbara Debbie Mildred Darold Henry Lucy Leveta Jack Dylan Ashley Claudio Susanne Carmen Sandra Nelle Jane Dee David Terri Marti Janet Gordon Sienna Alisha Kristi Julian Genevieve Kellen Crystal Carla Landon Sarah Rhonda Gail Travis Beverly Maxine Windlan Lynne Lance Curt Max Joe Tre'Vaughn Madeline Hercules Ruby Ali Laurie Cher Alex Michael Abdul Andy Jasmine Tameia Ka'Mel Jose John Jeremy Patrick Kristen Francoise Shemeika Cecil Ralph Jennifer Megan Margaret Valerie Chelesa Sam Axel Carol Luke Tyreek Dotta Isaiah Paige Hunter Tatiyana Kyle Aaron Wayne Roli Judy Pam Mason Randy Jim Paula Brad Sheri Keith Scott Kayla Donna Beth Nika Michele Cindy Francine Becky Don Stan Jerry Truett Rita Holly Paulette Clayton Claire Lori Jase Jameson Brian Nora Frankie Morgan Jeff Chloe Isabel Miller Ipek Kathy Tonya Harvey Roger Sean Bridgette Megan Trudy Abbie Maren Pat Linda Mark Lucia Matthew Surin Tyler Tim Leslie Addy Colleen Bryce Campbell Lily Mary Burt Elissa Jason Lindsey Amelia Mike Dan Jordan Blake Rob Jennifer Lenny Katja Morgan Maddie Ally Seth Emmy Jada Brooke Ava Jake Izzy Ray Katlin Mace Cadence Payton Frances Gloria Virgil Heather Steve Sunny Johnny Cindy Ronnie Bill

You are showing common courtesy and respect to know his and her name.

GIVING RESPECT = GETTING RESPECT

7. Did you smile at…

your dad

a stranger

the cashier

YOUR MOM

your brother

your wife

your friends

your sister

your manager

your students

YOUR TEACHER

YOUR HUSBAND

I bet they smiled back.

When the weather suits you not, try smiling
When your coffee/hot chocolate isn't hot, try smiling
When your neighbors don't do right or your family all fight,
sure is hard but then you might try smiling

Doesn't change the things, of course, just smiling
But it cannot make them any worse, just smiling
And it seems to help your case, brightens up a gloomy place,
then it sort of rests your face—just smiling.

(Author Unknown)

8. Did you offer a helping hand without being asked?

Going the extra mile/kilometer is a way to show your commitment.

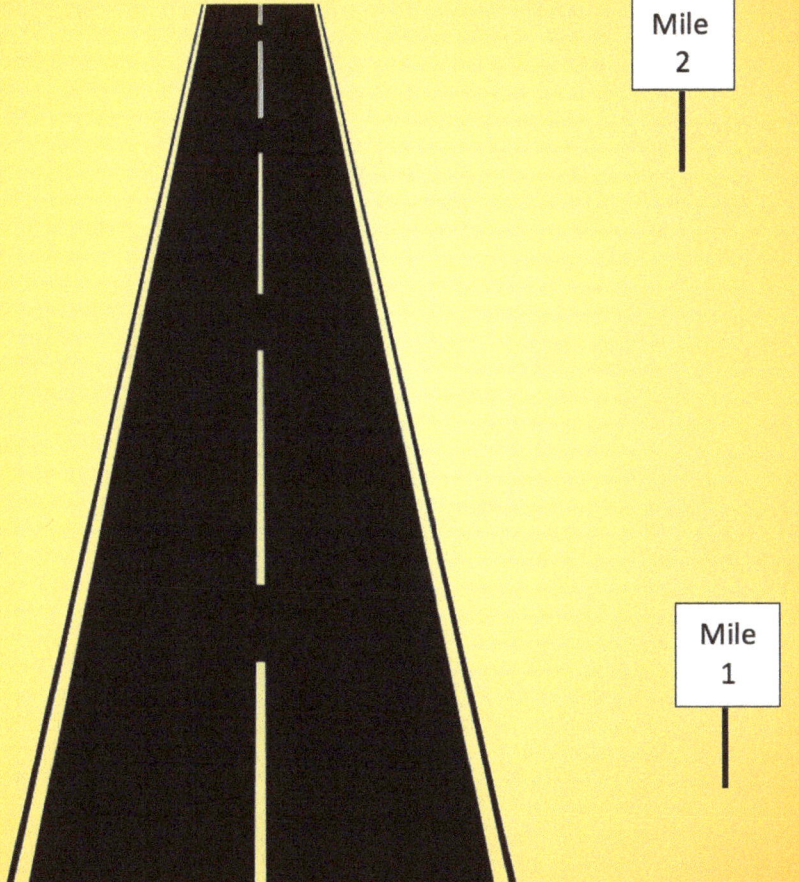

9. Did you pick up your clothes, toys, books; return messages; put the cap on the toothpaste; or put the toilet seat down?

????

Doing something you know others like is a way to show you care.

10. Did you do what you said you would do?

Pinky Promise

Keeping your word shows you respect others.

11. Did you use respectful language and an inside voice when speaking with others today?

🚫 Mean Words

🚫 Shouting

Being rude makes others feel bad.

12. Did you say "Stop it" to the person who was bullying another?

CYBER BULLYING

BULLYING

It is important to speak up when someone is being mistreated.

13. Did you put your cell phone, iPad, iPod, iTouch, Kindle, laptop, or electronic game away before sitting down for dinner or a meeting?

🚫 Cell phone   Laptop

Electronic game

iPad   Kindle   iTouch

Giving your undivided attention shows you are interested in what the other persons are saying.

14. Did you do your homework, assignment, project, and volunteer work without being prompted?

When you fulfill your obligations, you can learn new things and get tasks accomplished.

15. Did your behavior set a good example for others around you?

POSITIVE EXAMPLE

ROLE MODELS DO WHAT IS RIGHT

You can't wait until others behave appropriately. You control your actions.

16. Did you do the best you are capable of doing?

Second best is never what you should deliver.

17. Did you do what was right even when no one was looking?

It shouldn't matter who is looking. You do what you do because you know it is the right thing to do.

If it is wrong, it is wrong to do something even if everyone else is doing it. If it is right, it is right to do something even if no one else is doing it.

(St. Augustine of Hippo)

Quality means doing it right when no one is looking.

(Henry Ford)

18. Did you take criticism graciously?

Shhhhh
Constructive criticism in progress.

Accept feedback as a gift and thank the person for taking time to give it, even if you don't agree.

19. Did you listen with your ears, eyes, and heart?

It is easy to be distracted, and you can show the person you are listening, sincerely interested, by paying attention and being empathic.

EMPATHY

- ☺ Listen the way the other person would listen
- ☺ Show others you can see through their eyes
- ☺ Understand what it feels like to be in their shoes

20. Did you take time to show someone how to do something you do well?

It is a good use of your time and makes the other person know you want her or him to be successful.

21. Did you tell the whole truth?

LIAR, LIAR. PANTS ON FIRE.

It is always easier to remember what really happened than something you made up.

If you tell the truth, you don't have to remember anything

—Mark Twain

22. Did you try to exceed expectations?

Meeting your goals is expected, but exceeding your goals is a pleasant surprise.

23. Did you say "Please" or "Yes please"?

Por favor

Sila

S'il vous plâit

Bitte

Xin vin lòng

Mohon

Puhzhalsta

Responding politely shows you appreciate what the other person is doing for you.

APPRECIATE = Being grateful for something someone does for you and showing it

24. Did you try to catch someone doing something good?

Giving compliments is much more motivational than criticism.

I can live for two months on a good compliment.

—Mark Twain

25. Did you show compassion and kindness?

No act of kindness, no matter how small, is ever wasted.

—Aesop

When we demonstrate kindness and compassion to others, we are adding to our own happiness and physical/mental health. We grow five thousand new brain cells every day and positive actions can teach our brain to be more happy.

Folks are usually about as happy as they make their minds up to be.

—Abraham Lincoln

26. Did you consider how you could have done things differently when it didn't turn out like you wanted?

OOPS! OOPS!

We can learn from our mistakes if we take time to think about it.

MisTeaKs show we r tryin

27. Did you do something nice for someone else?

 Nice

 Bad

 Ugly

Giving your time and money to others releases chemicals in our brains that make us feel good.

Try to be a rainbow in someone's cloud.

—Maya Angelou

28. Did you forgive someone for something he/she did?

Holding on to negative feelings is harmful to your health and overall well-being.

Negative feelings = being nervous + being tense + loss of sleep + over/under eating + being mad at people

29. Did you laugh at your own mistakes?

Showing you know you messed up and acknowledging it was not a good thing to do is a way to show others you will try to do better next time. You may also give them a laugh.

We learn wisdom from failure much more than from success. We often discover what will do, by finding out what will not do; and probably he who never made a mistake never made a discovery

—Samuel Smiles

We all make mistakes. What we do afterward shows what kind of person we are.

30. Did you treat someone different from you in a nice way?

People are like snowflakes. Each one is different. Each one is special, and each one is beautiful. People who look different, speak different, worship different, or think different than you still want to be included.

What did you do to make someone smile?

> A smile costs nothing, but gives much. It enriches those who receive without making poorer those who give. It takes but a moment but the memory of it sometimes lasts forever. None is so rich or mighty that they can get along without it, and none is so poor that they can be made rich by it. A smile creates happiness in the home, fosters good will in business, and is the countersign of friendship. It brings rest to the weary, cheer to the discouraged, sunshine to the sad, and it is nature's best antidote for trouble. Yet it cannot be bought, begged, borrowed, or stolen, for it is given away. Some people are too tired to give you a smile. Give them one of yours, as none needs a smile so much as they who have no more to give.
>
> *Author Unknown*

Author's Page

Vicki Ellis Hargrove is a seasoned human resource professional, business consultant, educator, and Recognition Professionals International Certified Recognition professional. She grew up in Murray, Kentucky, and graduated from Murray State University with her bachelor and master degrees. She received her PhD from The Ohio State University in Columbus, Ohio, USA.

She was responsible for the global roll out of a corporate innovation system and electronic performance management tool in a large corporation of 150,000 employees in sixty countries. She served on the corporate-wide recognition advisory committee responsible for two company recognition events, recognition website, and documentation for the organization's recognition best practices. She provided leadership coaching for the front line to the executive level manager and led business improvement teams.

She is active in Recognition Professionals International (RPI) and serves as chair of the Product Development team and a member of the Board of Directors. She has facilitated and assisted in designing their recognition certification courses and has received a Spotlight Award and the Harkins-Howell Excellence in Education Award for her RPI service.

She has a son, a daughter-in-law, and two grandchildren in Florida and a stepdaughter in Texas. Her husband is a former schoolteacher and coach.

Together they like to travel, golf, and participate in family activities. They currently live in Jacksonville, Florida, USA.

Dr. Hargrove wrote *The Smile Experience* to accompany *Make Someone Smile* as a workbook and action planner to help you make others happy. She also wrote *The Adventures of Scout*, which is about her beloved and naughty black lab. Her books are available in e-format and traditional format from Amazon.

"What did you do to make someone smile?" has been a question Vicki regularly asks her grandchildren.

Who will you ask?

Milton Keynes UK
Ingram Content Group UK Ltd.
UKHW020939301123
433498UK00011B/221